20 Historical Black Natives of Charleston, South Carolina: Volume One

20 Historical Black Natives of Charleston, South Carolina: Volume One

RICHARD P.D. WARREN SR.

RICHARD P.D. WARREN SR.
2020

First Printing: 2020

ISBN 978-0-359-92882-8

Richard P.D. Warren Sr.
Charleston, South Carolina

Dedication

To our children, youth, and forthcoming generations:

may you always be inspired to create a glorious future that is as great and beautiful as YOU are!

I challenge you to learn & never forget the meaning of the Red, Black, and Green colors of our Pan-African flag (designed by the honorable Marcus Mosiah Garvey & officially adopted on August 13, 1920). These colors will always remind you of both your purpose and identity!

Contents

Alice Childress was born in Charleston, South Carolina, on October 12, 1916.

Occupation: Novelist, Playwright, and Actress

Notable Facts:
- She is recognized as the only African American woman to have written, produced, and published plays for approximately forty years.

- Alice Childress's 1952 play "Gold through the Trees" is the first professionally produced play by an African American woman.

- She was a crucial figure in the Harlem Renaissance.

Alonzo Jacob Ransier was born a "Free Person of Color" in Charleston, South Carolina, on January 3, 1834.

Occupation: Politician

Notable Facts:
- He was South Carolina's first African American Lieutenant Governor.

- Alonzo J. Ransier served as a member of the U.S. House of Representatives from South Carolina's 2nd district.

- During his time in Congress, he fought for the Civil Rights Act of 1875.

Andrew Bryan was born in Goose Creek, South Carolina, during the year of 1737.

Occupation: Reverend/Preacher

Notable Facts:

- He founded the First Bryan Baptist Church (also affectionately called the "Mother Church of Black Baptists"/ "First African Baptist Church of Savannah") in Savannah, Georgia, on January 20, 1788.

- Andrew Bryan was imprisoned wrongfully for preaching to enslaved Africans and accused of planning a rebellion. He was released once trialed and found innocent.

- He purchased him and his family's freedom. Also, he eventually purchased the property site of the First Bryan Baptist Church for "30 pounds sterling" (approximately $150.00) during the year of 1793.

Archibald Henry Grimke was born on August 17, 1849, in Charleston, South Carolina.

Occupation: Lawyer, Author, Journalist, and Activist

Notable Facts:
- He was a successful graduate of freedmen's schools (Lincoln University and Harvard Law School).

- Archibald Grimke was one of the founders of the National Association for the Advancement of Colored People (NAACP) founded on February 12, 1909.

- In 1919, he was awarded the Spingarn Medal for his life work for racial equality by the NAACP.

Benjamin M. Holmes was born in Charleston, South Carolina, in 1846.

Occupation: Teacher, News Correspondent, Singer

Notable Facts:
- Benjamin M. Holmes attended Fisk University.

- During his time at Fisk University, he joined the school's choir, which became known as the Jubilee Singers.

- After his time at Fisk University, he spent a year teaching the children of former enslaved African-Americans in one-room schoolhouses.

Bernice Violanthe Robinson was born in Charleston, South Carolina, on February 7, 1914.

Occupation: Cosmetologist, Civil Rights Activist, Educator

Notable Facts:
- She owned a beauty salon in Charleston. She would often use the space as a meeting place for politicians and fellow activists.

- Bernice Robinson was a member of the local National Association for the Advancement of Colored People (NAACP) branch in Charleston.

- She worked directly with Esau Jenkins and her cousin Septima Poinsette Clark during the Civil Rights Movement.

- Bernice Robinson is most known for establishing Citizenship Schools and registering African-American voters throughout the South.

Bertha "Chippie" Hill was born in Charleston, South Carolina, on March 15, 1905.

Occupation: Blues and Vaudeville Singer

Notable Facts:
- Bertha "Chippie" Hill started her dancing career at the age of 13 after her family relocated to New York City.

- By the year 1919, she was working with other performers such as Ethel waters and Ma Rainey.

- During the years 1925 and 1926, she recorded ten songs with the Okeh record company that featured Louis Armstrong.

Daniel Alexander Payne was born in Charleston, South Carolina, on February 24, 1811.

Occupation: Author, Educator, and Bishop

Notable Facts:
- Daniel Alexander Payne served as the sixth bishop for the African Methodist Episcopal Church (A.M.E.) from 1852 – 1893.

- In 1863 he became the first African American president of a university (Wilberforce University) in the United States.

- In 1865 he returned to the south to establish the A.M.E. denomination in Charleston (South Carolina) after the Civil War ended.

- The Payne elementary school in Washington, D.C., is named after him.

Edwin Augustus Harleston was born in Charleston, South Carolina, on March 14, 1882.

Occupation: Painter, Artist, and Civil Rights Leader

Notable Facts:
- He graduated from the Avery Normal Institute in 1900 and from Atlanta University in 1904.

- Edwin Harleston was the first president of Charleston's local National Association for the Advancement of Colored People (NAACP) Chapter.

- His artwork played a significant role during the Charleston Renaissance.

Ernest Everett Just was born in Charleston, South Carolina, on August 14, 1883.

Occupation: Biologist and Educator

Notable Facts:
- His first job after college was as a researcher and teacher at Howard University.

- Ernest E. Just, along with three Howard University juniors, founded the Omega Psi Phi fraternity on November 17, 1911.

- He obtained a Doctor of Philosophy degree from the University of Chicago.

- Ernest E. Just wrote two books and published at least 70 papers regarding different biology topics.

- He was the first person from America to be invited to the Kaiser Wilhelm Institute in Berlin-Dahlem, Germany.

Esau Jenkins was born on Johns Island, South Carolina, on July 3, 1910.

Occupation: Civil Rights Activist, African-American Human Rights Leader, Businessman, and Community Organizer.

Notable Facts:
- Esau Jenkins started a Citizenship School that held workshops at the Progressive Club that was founded by him and other local families.

- In 1959, Esau Jenkins organized the Citizens' Committee of Charleston, which focused on the political, economic, and cultural improvement of African-Americans.

- In 1966 he founded the Community Owned Federal Credit Union (COFCU).

- During his lifetime, he owned a vegetable/fruit stand, motel, restaurant, and a fleet of buses in Charleston, South Carolina.

Frances Anne Rollin Whipper was born in Charleston, South Carolina circa 1845.

Occupation: Author, Teacher, Political Activist, Physician

Notable Facts:
- In 1865 she became a teacher for the Freedmen's Bureau in Charleston.

- Frances Anne Rollin Whipper is the author of "Life and Public Services of Martin R. Delany (published in 1868 and became the first full-length biography written by an African American).

- She attended Howard University School of Medicine, where she became one of the first African-American women physicians in the United States.

Francis Lewis Cardozo was born in Charleston, South Carolina, on February 1, 1836.

Occupation: Educator, Politician

Notable Facts:
- In 1865 Francis Lewis Cardoza founded the Avery Normal Institute in Charleston. He became its second president from 1866 to 1868 (The Avery Normal Institute is now known as the Avery Research Center).

- Francis Lewis Cardozo became the first African American to hold a statewide office in the United States after being elected in South Carolina as Secretary of State in 1868.

- Francis Lewis Cardoza dedicated his entire life to opening doors to education for African American children.

George W. Prioleau was born in Charleston, South Carolina around 1856.

Occupation: U.S. Army Military Officer

Notable Facts:
- George Prioleau graduated from Wilberforce University with a Bachelor's Degree in Divinity.

- In 1895 George Prioleau became the chaplain of the 9th Cavalry of Buffalo Soldiers with the rank of Captain.

- He retired from the United States Army in 1920.

James Skivring Smith was born in Charleston, South Carolina, on February 26, 1825.

Occupation: Doctor, Physician and Politician

- **Notable Facts:**
  James Skivring Smith traveled with his parents to Liberia (Africa) in the year 1833.

- James Skivring Smith returned to the United States for college and graduated with his medical degree from Berkshire Medical College in 1848. He became the second African American to receive a Doctor of Medicine degree from an American medical school.

- After returning to Africa, James Skivring Smith served as the 6th President of Liberia from 1871 to 1872.

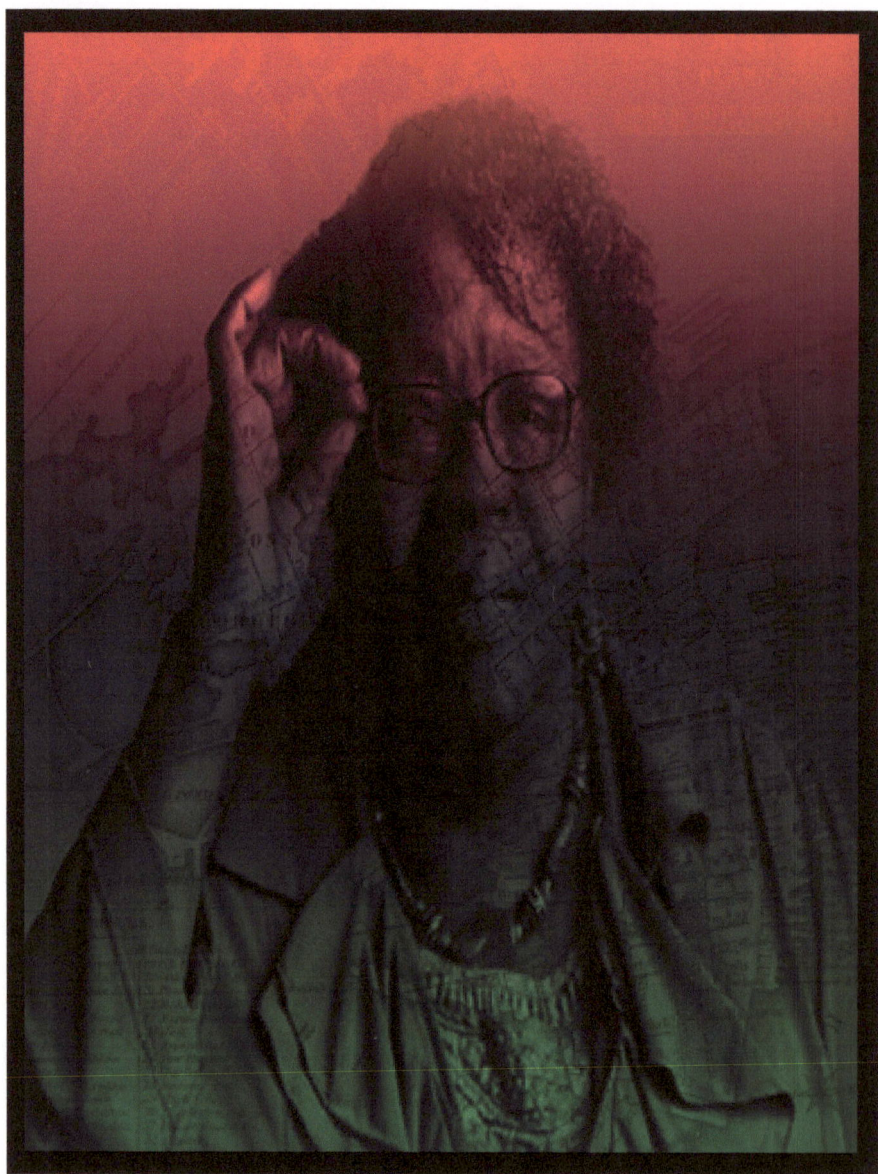

Mary Moultrie was born in Charleston, South Carolina during the year of 1943.

Occupation: Hospital Worker and Activist

Notable Facts:
- Mary Moultrie became a Licensed Practical Nurse (LPN) at the Goldwater Memorial Hospital in New York.

- In 1967 she returned to Charleston and was hired as a nurse assistant at the Medical University of South Carolina (MUSC).

- Mary Moultrie organized the Charleston Hospital Strike that lasted for 113 days (1968 – 1968), which resulted in a negotiated agreement that improved working conditions and increased workers' wages for African-American nurses.

Morris Brown was born on January 8, 1770 (or February 13, 1770), in Charleston, South Carolina.

Occupation: Shoemaker and Reverend

Notable Facts:
- In 1816 Morris Brown traveled to Philadelphia, Pennsylvania to work together with Rev. Richard Allen in the founding of America's first African Methodist Episcopal (AME) Church.

- Morris Brown founded the African Methodist Episcopal Church in Charleston, South Carolina (later named the Emmanuel AME Church).

- The Morris Brown Church in Charleston, South Carolina and the historic Morris Brown College in Atlanta, Georgia are both named after him.

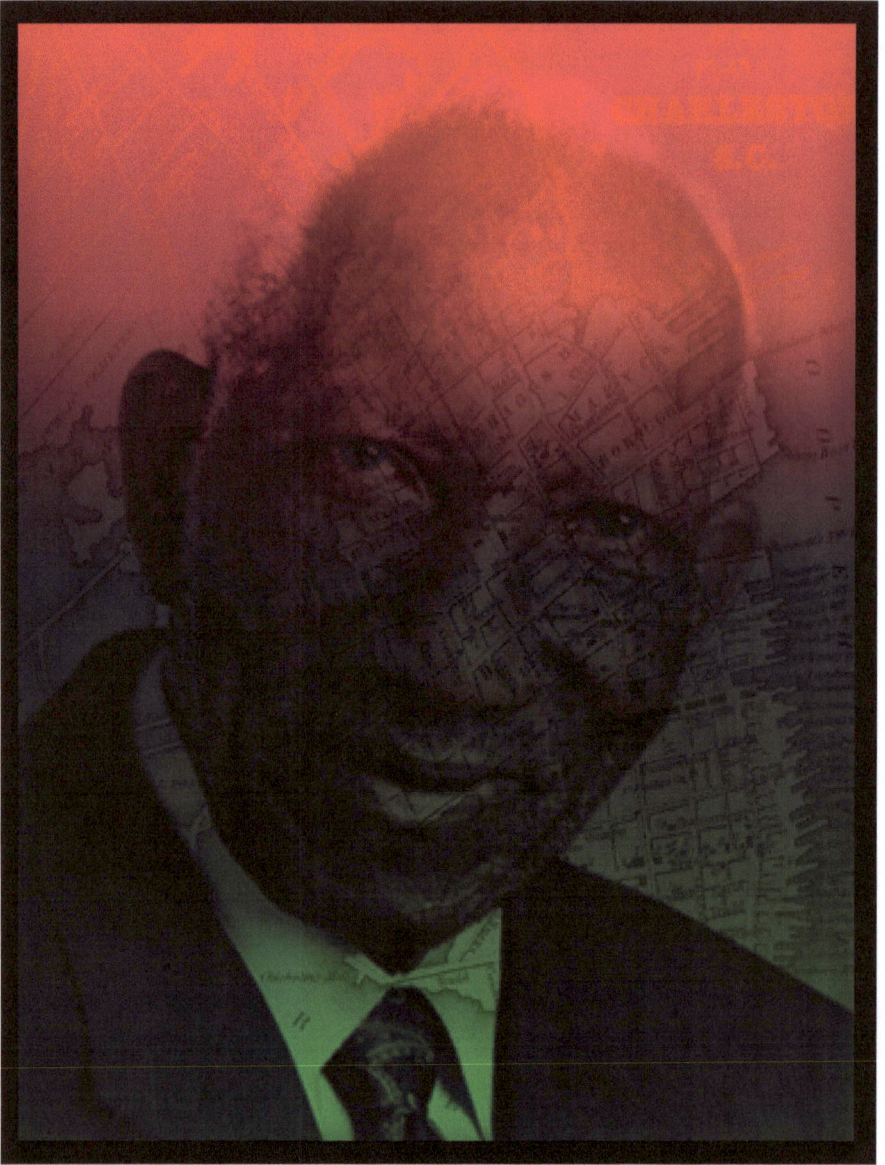

Philip Simmons was born on Daniel Island, Charleston, South Carolina, on June 9, 1912.

Occupation: Artisan and Blacksmith

Notable Facts:
- Philip Simmons was a Blacksmith for 78 years.

- During his career, Philip Simmons created over 500 pieces of artwork included iron fences, gates, balconies, and more that can be seen in Charleston and throughout the Low Country.

- Philip Simmons obtained many awards, such as the National Endowment for the Arts/National Heritage Fellowship, Lifetime Achievement Award, Order of the Palmetto, and more.

- In 1994 Philip Simmons was added to the South Carolina Hall of Fame.

Samuel David Ferguson was born in Charleston, South Carolina, on January 1, 1842.

Occupation: Reverend and Bishop

Notable Facts:
- Samuel David Ferguson was the first African-American elected as an Episcopal Church Bishop in Liberia, Africa.

- In 1889 Samuel David Ferguson established the Cuttington University in Cape Palmas (Liberia, Africa).

- In 1905 Samuel David Ferguson founded the Julia C. Emery Hall near Clay-Ashland (Liberia, Africa).

Septima Poinsette Clark was born in Charleston, South Carolina, on May 3, 1898.

Occupation: Educator and Civil Rights Activist

Notable Facts:
- Septima Poinsette Clark is known as the Grandmother/Queen Mother of the Civil Rights Movement in the United States.

- Septima Poinsette Clark graduated from college twice, receiving her bachelor's degree from Benedict College and her master's degree from Hampton Institute.

- Septima Poinsette Clark obtained the position of vice president of Charleston's local National Association for the Advancement of Colored People (NAACP) branch in 1956.

- Septima Poinsette Clark dedicated years of her life to establishing "Citizenship Schools" throughout the South.

- During her lifetime, Septima Poinsette Clark wrote two autobiographies: *Echo In My Soul* (1962) and *Ready from Within* (1979).

- In Charleston, South Carolina the Septima P. Clark Parkway (also known as the Septima P. Clark Expressway) and the Septima P. Clark Memorial Park are both named in her honor.

DANIEL JENKINS

ROBERT SMALLS

MORE NAMES TO REMEMBER:

Below is a shortlist of historical figures born outside of Charleston, South Carolina but still made a historical impact in the city during their lifetime.

Daniel Jenkins: Daniel Jenkins founded the Jenkins Orphanage in Charleston, South Carolina during the year of 1892, which became the first and only orphanage in the city for the African-American community in Charleston.

Denmark Vesey: Denmark Vesey organized a significant rebellion plan known as the Denmark Vesey's conspiracy of 1822 to liberate the enslaved African-American community in Charleston.

Gullah Jack: Gullah Jack was a co-conspirator of the Denmark Vesey's conspiracy of 1822, he played the significant role of recruiting many of the African soldiers.

Robert Smalls: Robert Smalls freed him, his family, and other enslaved Africans from slavery by piloting a confederate ship and sailing it out of Charleston in 1862.

Jemmy Cato: Jemmy Cato led a rebellion known as the "Stono Rebellion" on the banks of the Stono River on September 9, 1739, to liberate himself and as many enslaved Africans as possible.

www.ingramcontent.com/pod-product-compliance
Lightning Source LLC
Chambersburg PA
CBHW042126080426
42734CB00001B/19